DAVID COLBERT

10 DAYS

ABRAHAM LINCOLN

ALADDIN PAPERBACKS

NEW YORK LONDON TORONTO SYDNEY

ALADDIN PAPERBACKS • An imprint of Simon & Schuster Children's Publishing Division • 1230 Avenue of the Americas, New York, NY 10020 • Copyright © 2009 by David Colbert • Thanks to John Chew for his mathematical expertise • All illustrations, woodcuts, and photographs courtesy of the Library of Congress • All rights reserved, including the right of reproduction in whole or in part in any form. • ALADDIN PAPERBACKS and related logo are registered trademarks of Simon & Schuster, Inc. • Designed by Karin Paprocki • The text of this book was set in Perpetua. • Manufactured in the United States of America • First Aladdin Paperbacks edition January 2009
10 9 8 7 6 5 4 3 2
Library of Congress Control Number 2008937174
ISBN-13: 978-1-4169-6807-8
ISBN-10: 1-4169-6807-5

CONTENTS

INTRODUCTION
Denounced as unpatriotic for his belief in democracy, then nominated for high office almost as an afterthought, Lincoln became the country's most admired president.

DAY 1:
OCTOBER 5, 1818
ALONE
A childhood tragedy makes Lincoln wonder about leaving his mark on the world.

DAY 2:
JANUARY 12, 1848
UNPOPULAR VOICE
Lincoln sacrifices his first national office to speak out against a war and a president.

DAY 3:
NOVEMBER 2, 1858
THE GOOD FIGHT
Lincoln debates Senator Stephen A. Douglas about the extension of slavery into the American West.

INTRODUCTION

The people who rise to the top aren't always the heroes their biographies make them out to be. Abraham Lincoln, however, has become the gold standard by which other presidents are judged, and by which many of them judge themselves. Historians and the general public almost always place him in the top spot when presidents are ranked.

Yet during his lifetime, Lincoln was called unpatriotic and even a tyrant. When he was elected to the presidency, members of his own party questioned his ability. During the war, his judgment was questioned. Afterward, a large part of the population hated him.

To a large extent, we revere him now because we live in a world he helped to create. We're taught and believe, as he believed, that Americans should enjoy equal rights and status under the law. We believe that the government of the United States derives its authority from the people, and exists to serve them.

These may seem like simple and obvious ideas, almost too childish to mention in our modern, complex world; but in Lincoln's lifetime there were serious doubts that people could govern themselves. Lincoln was born in 1809, less than thirty years after the American Revolution ended, and just twenty years after the Constitution established our present form of government (the presidency, Congress, and the Supreme Court.) That early period in the country's history was marked by many disputes among the states and between the states and the federal government.

Throughout Lincoln's life, the countries of Europe still expected the American experiment with democracy to end in chaos. The Civil War was seen by some as the final breakdown.

Although Lincoln's simple ideals were ridiculed by his political opponents and by his rivals within his own party, he stuck to them at a time when other politicians became lost in complexity. That's an important reason Lincoln's vision of the country has prevailed. What's far less simple is the route Lincoln took to reach his goals. "I claim not to have controlled events," he said, "but confess plainly that events have controlled me." Though he was being too modest, there's some truth in that statement, even when it comes to his most admired achievement, the end of slavery.

If people know nothing else about the Civil War, they know it ended slavery. If they know only one thing about Lincoln, it's that he freed the slaves. But those one-line versions of history focus on the final results of a process that took place over many years and could have moved in many different directions.

Lincoln, like the country, moved step by small step toward the end of slavery. Had the South not split from the United States and attacked it, Lincoln might not have used his presidential power to abolish slavery. Although he very much wanted slavery to end, he also believed the Constitution and other laws protected it where it already existed. Even during the Civil War there were slave states in the Union—Delaware, Maryland, Kentucky, Missouri, and West Virginia. Lincoln offered to pay the slave owners of those states if they would free their slaves, and worked hard to get them to agree, but when they refused he didn't impose his will on them. He believed, probably correctly, they'd try to join the Confederacy if he forced his wishes on them.

Even his famous Emancipation Proclamation didn't free those Union slaves. It had effect only in the Confederate territory then under control of the U.S. Army. In what now may seem like an unusual twist of history but at the time was a tragedy, slavery existed in the Union states of the North until several months after the Civil War had freed the slaves of the South.

The complicated path to some simple ideas is what this book is about. It doesn't contain many of the fun stories that have become standard for biographies of Lincoln: He was a great wrestler, he could really swing an axe, and he grew a beard because a young girl asked him to do it. It's about the larger questions facing the country during his lifetime, and the answers Lincoln offered. In the ten days of his 20,517 described in the chapters that follow, the ten that most changed his life and yours, the changing fortunes of two rival armies may mean less than the change that took place in the minds of most Americans.

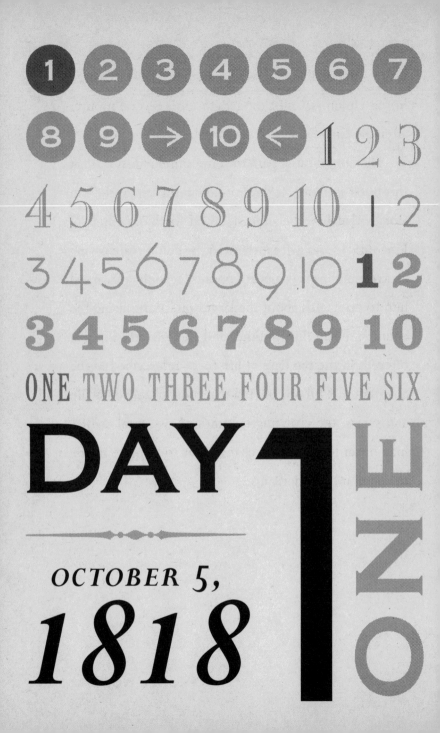

ALONE

Near Little Pigeon Creek, Indiana.

ine-year-old Abraham Lincoln and his eleven-year-old sister, Sarah, are choking back tears as they sit on the wooden steps outside the family's log home. Inside, their mother, Nancy Hanks Lincoln, is ill and dying. She's contracted "milk sickness," a mysterious disease that's sweeping their small community in the Indiana wilderness. It gets its name because people seem to catch it from drinking milk. Victims feel dizzy and vomit a lot, then slowly slip into a coma and die. Animals are also catching it and dying. Nancy Lincoln's aunt and uncle have already died in the last two weeks.

The Lincoln family was leading a difficult life even before Nancy Lincoln became ill. Living in what was then part of America's western frontier, in a community of only about forty families within a five-mile range of their cabin, they are surviving, not thriving. Lincoln's father, a carpenter by trade who does a little farming, endured a bleak frontier childhood, and has been unable to raise himself from those circumstances. He has no education and has difficulty signing his own name. He has already tried his luck with a couple of farms in Kentucky, where Abraham was born, before he moved the family to Indiana.

Lincoln's mother, however, is an extraordinary woman with education and talents far surpassing her husband's. Her background is a mystery, and remains a mystery still to historians. She was raised by a single mother. Her father, some evidence suggests, was a

This log cabin was the last home of Lincoln's father. Abraham's boyhood home was probably even more rustic, and smaller.

member of Virginia's highest social class, already married and with a family, which would explain why his relationship to Nancy was a secret.

Although the mysterious circumstances of her birth placed her on the fringes of society because of the morals of the time, and meant that she grew up poor, her intellect and determination are widely admired. A childhood friend of Lincoln later recalls the "extraordinary strength of her mind," adding that she was "superior to her husband in every way . . . a brilliant woman." Others who know her describe her the same way. Lincoln's father is considered lucky to have married her. Just as she taught him how to sign his name, she later teaches Abraham and Sarah how to read and write, and passes on her determination to gain an education despite the family's isolation in the wilderness. She will also pass along a political ideal: The family had moved from Kentucky to Indiana "partly on account of slavery," Lincoln will later explain. Kentucky was a slave state; Indiana was not. (They had already changed religious congregations because of their antislavery views.)

Many years from this sad day, Lincoln will tell a friend, "All that I am or hope ever to be I get from my mother, God bless her." Although he is referring to her intelligence and willingness to work hard, his comment is also true in another and possibly more important way. The loss of his mother at such an early age—both his and hers—seems to have had a profound effect on his personality. Naturally, he feels great loneliness. This feeling will never truly leave him, even in later years when he has many friends. Also, the sudden nature of his mother's passing instills in him worries about an early death of his own—an eerie premonition of the future.

Ironically, both of these tragic changes will benefit the nation. His long experience with solitude, with thinking through difficult questions and feelings on his own, will later strengthen him enough to make difficult decisions as president, even when his advisers recommend an easy way out. But most important of all, the shocking speed with which his mother seemed to be erased from history fuels his desire to leave a

ABOUT TWENTY YEARS AFTER THE DEATH OF LINCOLN'S MOTHER, A DOCTOR WILL FIGURE OUT THAT MILK SICKNESS IS CAUSED WHEN ANIMALS FEED ON A POISONOUS PLANT. THE ANIMAL ITSELF DOESN'T DIE, BUT ITS MILK CARRIES THE TOXIN.

permanent and positive mark on the world. Later he will admit to friends that he has no faith in the existence of a heavenly afterlife. For him, what mattered was what a person did on Earth.

Unfortunately, these feelings will only be reinforced about ten years from this day, when his sister Sarah dies in childbirth—another sudden loss, and another horrible shock.

By then, however, Abraham will already have shown he's capable of putting desire into action. Despite having less than a year of formal schooling because he has to work so much, he teaches himself from every book he can borrow, from *Aesop's Fables* to volumes of state law. He owns very few books, but he has some book with him all the time, tucked under his arm or by his side. He dips into it whenever he has a few spare moments. If he finds a passage he likes, he memorizes it by writing it over and over again, sometimes using a piece of coal on a board of wood if he has no pencil or paper.

He's encouraged by his stepmother, who his father will marry about a year from this day. Also named Sarah—Sarah Bush Johnston Lincoln—she's a widow with children of her own. However, she loves Abraham like a son. She knows right away he's "a boy of uncommon natural talents." She's aware she's not the intellectual equal of Nancy Lincoln, nor even of Abraham, but she does what she can to help him with his education. They get along very well—better than Abraham gets along with his father, who would rather Abraham stick to chopping wood and plowing fields. She would later say about Abraham that, "his mind & mine—what little I had—seemed to run together, [to] move in the same channel."

Both of them understood that the channel in which Lincoln's mind ran pointed out—away from the frontier, where so many Americans were heading to create new lives. Lincoln had seen enough of the freedom and opportunity that individuals gained when they moved to the frontier. He respected the

At left is Sarah Bush Johnston Lincoln, Abraham's stepmother.
At right is his father Thomas. (No genuine portraits of Lincoln's
mother Nancy are yet known to exist.) Lincoln and his father didn't
get along well, and as adults were not close. But Abraham's
affection for his stepmother lasted throughout his life.
He continued to visit her after his father's death, including
just before his first inauguration as president in 1861.
Sarah died in 1869, four years after Abraham.

people who followed that dream, and considered the freedom to do so an essential part of American life. But for him, leaving his mark meant living in a larger world of people.

He might have done the same thing even if his

mother had survived this tragic day in 1818, but he certainly wouldn't have been the same man, and events will soon show that his character, so deeply formed by this day, is what will matter most when his own opportunities come. ❶

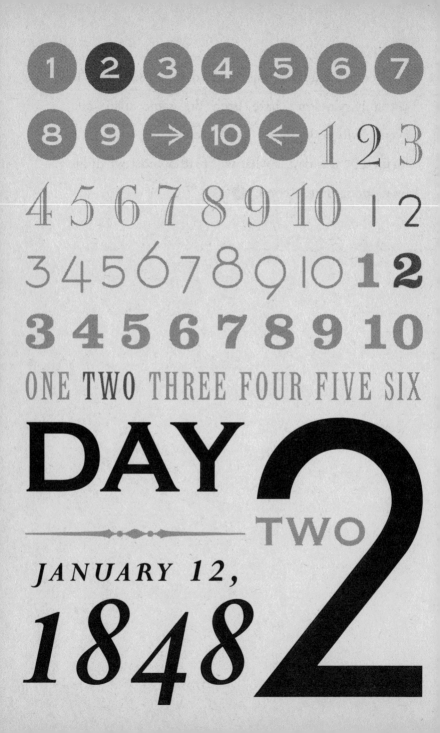

UNPOPULAR VOICE

Washington DC.

Lincoln, almost thirty-nine years old, has finally achieved a goal he has had for a long time: After some unsuccessful attempts, his district in Illinois has elected him to the U.S. House of Representatives.

Most politicians in that position play it safe. New members of Congress are told to act like children—*Be seen but not heard*—and Lincoln, having waited so long for his chance to play a role in national affairs,

Lincoln in his late thirties. It's believed this photo was taken in 1846 or 1847, although Lincoln's oldest son, Robert, thought it might have been taken a year or so later, when Lincoln was serving in Congress.

has every reason to be cautious, polite, and politically correct. Instead, today Lincoln will launch a political attack on the party that controls Congress, and on the president of the United States, James K. Polk.

The Illinois voters who sent him to Washington—many of whom knew him from his four previous terms as a state legislator—will be surprised. He's not known as a firebrand. He's seen as good-natured, and more likely to make his point with a funny story than a long speech. He still displays the social graces of a frontier American, which pleases his supporters. His intellect and judgment are well-regarded, but he's modest about them. During his terms in the Illinois legislature, he focused on dull but important improvements to the state's roads and waterways.

But unlike many good-natured politicians who appear confident and powerful yet constantly worry about losing anyone's goodwill, Lincoln isn't afraid to take a stand against popular opinion. While he was a state legislator, someone called for a vote supporting the "right of property in slaves." Because Illinois was a northern, free state, it was just a symbolic vote favoring the policies of slavery, not a vote for a law. Voting "aye," which was how most of the public felt, would have cost Lincoln nothing. In fact, of the eighty-two other legislators voting on the bill, only five were voting against it. But Lincoln joined the tiny group making a stand against the bill, going on record with his unpopular belief that "the institution of slavery is founded on both injustice and bad policy." This is the Lincoln who is about to make a stand in Congress.

THE WAR PATH

T he issue for him today isn't slavery; it's war. For the past two years, the United States has been fighting Mexico, because Mexico owns land that the United States wants. A few years earlier, in 1845, the United States announced it was taking over the Mexican territory of Texas. Around the same time, it told Mexico it wanted to buy the territories of California and New Mexico. But Mexico said it wanted Texas back, and that it wasn't interested in

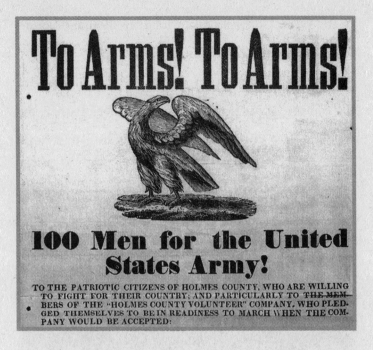

A recruiting poster for the Mexican-American War

selling the other land. That's when the United States decided to take the land by force. Claiming that Mexico had attacked Americans in Texas—a claim that historians consider questionable—the federal government, driven by President Polk, roused the country with slogans about liberty and justice for the people of the West. Congress asked for fifty thousand volunteers; three hundred thousand signed up.

From the declaration of war in May of 1846 to the capture of Mexico City in September of 1847, the war was easy going for the United States. It secured

James K. Polk (1795–1849), the eleventh president of the United States. Son of a wealthy farmer, and a distinguished student at the University of North Carolina, he was a member of Congress by age thirty, then Speaker of the House of Representatives, and then governor of Tennessee before becoming president. Although his critics, including Lincoln, disliked his tactics for expanding the borders of the U.S., within his own party he was considered moderate because he didn't want to take all of Mexico.

everything it wanted. Military commanders became national heroes. When Lincoln arrived in Washington as a new member of Congress, all that remained was negotiation of the final peace treaty.

Incredibly, Lincoln is going to make a principled protest against the war. The past two years have proved that war critics are shouted down and called unpatriotic. Even the colleagues who agree with him believe he's making a mistake by speaking publicly about the subject.

But for Lincoln, the issue is too important to ignore. Ulysses S. Grant, the future general and U.S. president, was a young officer in Mexico and was angry about the war until the end of his life: "To this day," he said shortly before dying, "I regard the war . . . as one of the most unjust ever waged by a stronger against a weaker nation. It was an instance of a republic following the bad example of European monarchies, in not considering justice in their desire to acquire additional territory."

War critics had another crucial objection: As Grant put it, "The occupation, separation and annexation [of Texas] were, from the inception of the movement to its final consummation, a conspiracy to acquire territory out of which slave states might be formed for the American Union." Although extending slavery would have broken several agreements made between the states—one of which, the Northwest Ordinance of 1787, was older than the Constitution—the slave states didn't care.

A congressman from Pennsylvania, David Wilmot, tried to prevent this extension of slavery by making Congress agree even before the war ended that slavery would not be permitted in any territory gained during the conflict. Congress rejected this "Wilmot Proviso" many times.

President Polk, of course, consistently told the public that taking territory had never been the goal of the United States. He completely avoided the question of slavery. Lincoln was infuriated by Polk's dishonesty in explaining the reasons for, and goals of, the war. A few days before this day's confrontation, Lincoln demanded evidence from Polk for the president's claim that Mexico was the aggressor. On this day, he'll be even stronger in his attack.

"MISERABLY PERPLEXED"

Washington DC has forty thousand residents—an astonishing number to a westerner like Lincoln. But the city still has only two paved streets, and the backyards of even downtown houses are likely to be filled with farm animals. Heading to the Capitol Building, which doesn't yet have its distinctive dome, Lincoln passes pigs that have been let out to feed on street litter.

He's fired up by the time he rises to make his speech. The careful, moderate words for which he'll eventually become famous are set aside today. He says

A political cartoon from 1848 makes fun of Senator Lewis Cass,
a nominee for president who wanted to continue the expansionist
policies of President Polk. He's saying, "New Mexico, California,
Chihuahua, Zacatecas, Mexico, Peru, Yucatan, Cuba"—the first two
being territories just won in the war with the Mexico, the others
being what he'd supposedly take next. The bloody sword over his
head, labelled "Manifest Destiny," refers to the idea that European
Americans had an obvious ("manifest") fate ("destiny") to expand
westward across the continent. Cass lost the election.

the president's reason for going to war was "the sheerest deception." Polk's latest explanations, Lincoln says,

are "like the half insane mumbling of a fever-dream." The President's ever-changing plans to finish what was started, says Lincoln, are "equally wandering and indefinite." Unusually for Lincoln, it's a strong personal attack: Polk, Lincoln says, "knows not where he is. He is a bewildered, confounded, and miserably perplexed man."

Much of what Lincoln says is true, but that hardly matters. The label of "unpatriotic" is easily stuck to war protesters, even when they're right. Few voters will stop to think that Lincoln was actually being more patriotic than they were. (Another Illinois politician of the time refused to voice his opinions against the Mexican-American with a sarcastic comment about the public's love of war: "I opposed [the War of 1812]. That was enough for me. I am now perpetually in favor of war, pestilence, and famine.") Although Lincoln's term in Congress is only just beginning, he has already made enemies and disappointed voters back in Illinois. When his term is over, his party will lose his seat and Lincoln's criticism of the war will be blamed, with good reason.

In the end, the United States will pay Mexico for much of the land it has taken, which will make the critics happy. But the question of slavery in the new territories won't be resolved. The conflict in the West will soon turn deadly, foreshadowing the Civil War. When it does, Lincoln will be there. **2**

Gold was discovered in the newly won territory of California less than a month before the signing of the treaty ending the Mexican-American War. The Gold Rush began about a year later, and in time Americans outnumbered the Mexican citizens of the state. The poster above advertises "The Quickest, Safest and Cheapest" passage in the days before the railroad: Two steamship rides connected by an overland passage in Central America, where the Atlantic and Pacific oceans are separated by only a couple of hundred miles. The company advertising in this poster has a route through Nicaragua. Panama was a more popular choice.

THE GOOD FIGHT

Springfield, Illinois.

Lincoln will later remember this evening as "dark, rainy and gloomy." The weather might not have bothered the forty-nine-year-old lawyer so much if he had won the election held this day, but, despite all his efforts, he has been defeated.

The winner, Stephen A. Douglas, will return to Washington for another term as an Illinois senator. Although Illinois is a free state, its position as a gateway to the American West makes the question of slavery in the new states and territories important to its citizens. Today's vote centered on it.

Douglas supports slavery. When his late wife inherited a family plantation, Douglas took over its management, and he has continued in that role. (Though for political appearances he has never held direct ownership of the slaves, they are effectively his.) Following the Mexican-American war, as chairman of the Senate's Committee on Territories, he helped craft the Compromise of 1850, a set of laws that required northern states to return escaped slaves, and which allowed the residents of some of the western territories to decide for themselves if they wanted slavery. Four years later he shepherded the Kansas-Nebraska Act, which gave voters in those territories the right to decide if they wanted slavery. Of course, slaves weren't allowed to vote. (Neither were women.)

After the Kansas-Nebraska Act was passed, Lincoln, like many others with a strong antislavery position,

Stephen A. Douglas (1813–1861). Historian Albert Bushnell Hart said, "Douglas was a masterful man of great intellectual power, indomitable energy, shrewdness in forming political combinations, and little scruple [morality]. He was probably the only man in Congress who would have ventured or could have carried through the Kansas-Nebraska bill, a voluntary offering to the south by a northern Democrat."

joined a new political party, the Republicans. A few months before this evening, Illinois Republicans nominated Lincoln as their candidate for the U.S. Senate.

Lincoln accepted the nomination with a speech that has become famous. His "House Divided" speech alluded to a Bible passage (Matthew 12:25) that reads, "Every kingdom divided against itself is brought to desolation; and every city or house divided against itself shall not stand."

A house divided against itself cannot stand. I believe this government cannot endure, permanently, half slave and half free. I do not expect the Union to be dissolved—I do not expect the house to fall—but I do expect it will cease to be divided. It will become all one thing or all the other. Either the opponents of slavery will arrest the further spread of it, and place it where the public mind shall rest in the belief that it is in the course of ultimate extinction; or its advocates will push it forward, till it shall become alike lawful in all the States, old as well as new—North as well as South.

Mary Todd Lincoln (1818–1882), Abraham Lincoln's wife. From a wealthy and prominent Kentucky family that had many political connections, her energy and uninhibited spirit were apparent from childhood. She moved to Springfield, the capital of Illinois, when she was about twenty, and was courted by several distinguished men, including Abraham Lincoln's future political rival, Stephen A. Douglas. The Civil War caused her to be separated from part of her family, which lived in the South, and she became increasingly anxious, but she and Abraham remained devoted to each other even when she developed what seems to be a mental illness. This photograph is believed to have been taken while she was First Lady, some time between 1860 and 1865.

Its advocates will push it forward, till it shall become alike lawful in all the States. Lincoln knew that many people who opposed slavery believed it would disappear by itself if were left alone. This was wishful thinking. The Founding Fathers had fooled themselves into believing it when they wrote the Constitution. They hoped it might last just another twenty years, to 1808, by which time new waves of immigrant labor from Europe would arrive to work on southern farms. They said no further slaves could be brought to the country after that date. But slavery persisted—as did the practice of looking the other way to maintain peace between the states.

Lincoln, too, had once hoped slavery would die on its own. But now he saw clearly that powerful men in the U.S. government were trying to make it law throughout the country. Along with Congress, both the president, James Buchanan, and the Supreme Court had recently shown a bias toward slavery. In the case of a slave named Dred Scott, who had been taken

Dred Scott

to the free state of Illinois for a long period and who had then claimed his freedom, the Supreme Court had ruled that slaves and their descendants were not and could never become citizens of the United States. They were property regardless of where in the United States they were. The court also ruled that Congress did not have the right under the Constitution to

*At left, Chief Justice of the Supreme Court Roger B. Taney;
at right, President James Buchanan*

restrict slavery, and that authorities in free states were
obliged to protect the property rights of slave owners.

President Buchanan was in sympathy with slave
owners. (His late household partner had been one.)
Ignoring the Constitution's separation of government
powers, Buchanan had worked with the chief justice of
the Supreme Court, Roger B. Taney, to craft the Dred
Scott decision and its public announcement. The Dred
Scott decision is now almost universally acknowledged

as a disgrace—an abomination of legal and human values. But when Lincoln debated Douglas, it was the law of the land.

"POPULAR SOVEREIGNTY"

In the months before this election night, the battle of ideas between Lincoln and Douglas became a national phenomenon. The two men held seven debates that were reported in newspapers across the country. These were huge events: Thousands of people came to hear the speakers, often traveling long distances by train. The campaign staffs of each man made sure their supporters showed up by arranging these excursions.

Douglas was a tough adversary. He presented himself as moderate which pleased the many undecided voters who simply wanted to avoid a civil war. All Douglas wanted, he said, was "popular sovereignty"—the rule of the people. Lincoln, said Douglas in one debate, "says that he looks forward to a time when slavery shall be abolished everywhere. I look forward to a time when each State shall be allowed to do as it pleases. If it chooses to keep slavery forever, it is not my business, but its own; if it chooses to abolish slavery, it is its own business—not mine. I care more for the great principle of self-government, the right of the people to rule, than I do for all the Negroes in Christendom."

Douglas made the solution of popular sovereignty sound like the best of American democracy. But he wasn't sincere. He didn't want people from the free states to vote on the question. He didn't want slaves to vote on it. Like nearly all politicians of the time, he also didn't want women to vote on it.

Douglas's limited idea of democracy had already led to extreme violence in Kansas following his Kansas-Nebraska Act. Thousands of people on both sides of the slavery issue had traveled to Kansas from surrounding states and territories to cast a vote on the issue. Where political tricks couldn't be used to keep the antislavery voters from the polls, proslavery terrorists did the job. (Although often called "guerrillas" in history books, the term "terrorist" is more accurate because civilians were targeted in addition to government forces.) A few antislavery men responded in kind. "Bleeding Kansas," as it came to be called, was actually an early battleground of what in a few years would formally become the Civil War.

The violence reached all the way to Washington DC. A senator from Massachusetts made a speech criticizing southerners for their role in the violence—a speech that included stupid and cruel comments about the physical disabilities of a senator from South Carolina who had suffered a stroke. A relative of the South Carolina senator, a congressman himself, approached the Massachusetts senator in the senate chamber and furiously beat his head with a cane until the cane broke. It was revenge for both the personal insult and the insult to South Carolina, the congress-man said. The injuries he'd inflicted were so severe that his victim would need three years to recover. Back home, the attacker was hailed as a hero. People sent him new canes as gifts.

Lincoln offered a simple reply to Douglas's insincere call for democracy: The heart of American democracy is stated clearly in the Declaration of Independence: "all men are created equal."

Douglas knew that most white people considered the equality of African Americans to be a ridiculous notion. Douglas derided Lincoln's views, saying:

> *Mr. Lincoln, following the example and lead of all the little Abolition orators, who go around and lecture in the basements of schools and churches, reads from the Declaration of Independence that all men were created equal. . . . I do not question Mr. Lincoln's conscientious belief that the Negro was made his equal, and hence is his brother; but*

for my own part, I do not regard the Negro as my equal, and positively deny that he is my brother, or any kin to me whatever.

Two debates later, he was even harsher:

I hold that a Negro is not and never ought to be a citizen of the United States. . . . Now, I say to you, my fellow-citizens, that in my opinion, the signers of the Declaration had no reference to the Negro whatever, when they declared all men to be created equal. They desired to express by that phrase white men, men of European birth and European descent, and had no reference either to the Negro, the savage Indians . . . or any other inferior and degraded race, when they spoke of the equality of men.

As repellent as these ideas are in the present day, Douglas was expressing what a large proportion of

Americans believed, and what the U.S. Supreme Court had said in the Dred Scott decision.

"ANOTHER EXPLOSION"

As the debates went on, Lincoln began to win support. Douglas then stooped to a tactic used many times before and since: He called Lincoln unpatriotic and a traitor because Lincoln had criticized the Mexican-American War:

> *It is one thing to be opposed to the declaration of a war, another and very different thing to take sides with the enemy against your own country after the war has been commenced. Our army was in Mexico at the time, many battles had been fought. . . . Lincoln's vote [was] sent to Mexico and read at the head of the Mexican army, to prove to them that there was a Mexican party in*

the Congress of the United States who were doing

all in their power to aid them.

Lincoln was no traitor, and Douglas knew it. But Douglas also knew that at least a few people would be easily fooled with that kind of attack. Still, Douglas's victory wasn't by a wide margin. His party won less than half the votes cast. (The voters weren't actually casting ballots directly for Lincoln and Douglas. They were choosing state legislators who would then choose between the two men.) Lincoln, though saddened by the results of this evening, is determined to press on. He sees no alternative for the country: The slavery advocates are asking for conflict by pushing their claims westward.

A few days from now he'll explain to a friend, "The fight must go on. The cause of civil liberty must not be surrendered at the end of one, or even, one hundred defeats. . . . Another explosion will soon come." ③

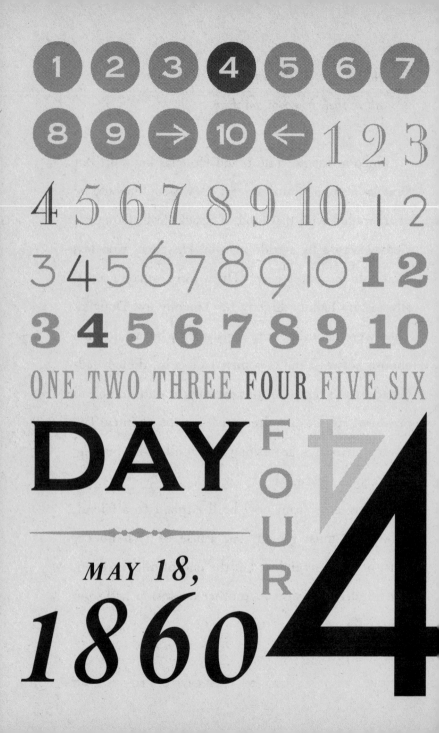

SURPRISE CANDIDATE

Chicago, Illinois.

The "Wigwam"—a new, large convention building—has been filling with excited men all morning. Although it's just after 9 a.m., thousands are inside, waiting to cast ballots to select the Republican Party's nominee for president. Many more wait outside for news. In all, forty thousand people have come to Chicago for the convention.

Four men are in the running. None of the experts believe Lincoln is the first choice of the majority.

Lincoln doesn't either. But knowing what he does about the other candidates, and about the party members who are voting, he believes he has a chance.

FOUR WINDS

The slavery issue has split many people from their old allegiances and led them to this new Republican Party. "Of strange, discordant, and even, hostile elements," Lincoln has said, "we gathered from the four winds, and formed and fought the battle through."

Lincoln's three rivals are New York Governor William H. Seward, Senator Salmon P. Chase of Ohio, and former Congressman Edward Bates of Missouri. In keeping with the practice of the time, none of the four are actually in Chicago. Each has a campaign manager in Chicago. Lincoln is back home in Springfield, Illinois, about two hundred miles away. The other

Inside the Wigwam during the convention

three candidates—each of whom is very confident of winning—are also in their home states.

Seward is the front-runner. A fiery orator, more than once he has announced his belief that a war over the slave question is inevitable. However, he's more moderate than many of his critics imagine. He's a practical politician who understands compromise.

Of all the candidates, Chase is the most committed to the immediate abolition of slavery everywhere.

The four main rivals at the 1860 Republican convention in Chicago. Clockwise from top left: Lincoln, the choice of moderates and the many local activists; Salmon P. Chase, the most radical opponent of slavery; William H. Seward, who was backed by a political machine with great influence; and Edward Bates, another moderate.

His state, Ohio, which, like Lincoln's Illinois, is a gateway to the West, has been a battleground in the slavery fight for many years. Chase has energetically used his great knowledge of law and politics to fight slavery's extension and to protect the rights of fugitive slaves.

Bates is the oldest of the candidates. Because he hasn't been involved in the most recent political battles that led to the creation of the party, and because his views are moderate, his supporters believe he's the best man to unite the different elements of the party.

Then there's Lincoln. His fighting spirit in the 1858 campaign against Stephen Douglas earned him supporters far beyond his home state of Illinois. About three months before the opening day of this convention, fifteen hundred people came to hear him speak at The Cooper Union, a college in New York City. His electrifying speech announced his belief that the proslavery South wanted to "destroy the government [of the United States]" unless it could interpret the Constitution as it pleased. The next day, the New York papers were full of praise for him, and he was asked to speak throughout the northeast of the country.

SECOND AMONG EQUALS

oing into the convention, Lincoln and his campaign manager, David Davis, have a simple strategy: Try to convince the supporters of each of the other candidates that Lincoln is the best second choice. They understand their opponents well. Seward and Chase have been fighting for the top position for so long that the supporters of each have built up a personal distaste for the other side. Although Bates appears to be a safe alternative to Seward or Chase, he proves there is such a thing as too safe: He hasn't distinguished himself with strong, clear positions as Lincoln has.

Lincoln's strategy begins to succeed after just the first round of voting: Seward 173 1/2; Lincoln

102; Chase 49; Bates 48. Lincoln is the alternative to Seward. By the second ballot, Lincoln's 181 votes are nearly equal to Seward's 184 1/2. By the third ballot, Lincoln has closed the gap to 1 1/2 votes—and when that figure is announced, a representative from Ohio stands up to announce that the last few holdouts for Chase will switch to Lincoln, eliminating the need for another round. The least likely candidate had won. When the news was announced outside the Wigwam, the mob, estimated to be between twenty thousand and thirty thousand people, began an all-night party. Within minutes, the news was telegraphed to Springfield and another celebration began there.

TEAMWORK

aturally, Lincoln's rivals were unhappy. Seward and Chase were crushed, angry, and resentful. Bates was disappointed and perplexed. Each imagined himself to be superior to Lincoln in intelligence and ability. Seward and Chase began to think ahead to the next presidential election, four years away. None of them understood Lincoln's ability to bring together people of different opinions and temperaments. He proved his skill, however, by beating all opponents and winning the national election in November. Almost immediately, Lincoln offered important cabinet posts to his rivals. Seward became secretary of state. Chase became secretary of the treasury. Bates became Attorney General. (A potential rival who had stepped aside before the voting began, Senator Simon Cameron of Pennsylvania, became Secretary of War.)

Lincoln's determination to put the best available person in each job, and to allow different opinions to exist in his government, was initially misunderstood by some people as a sign of weakness. Seward arrogantly suggested that Lincoln remain merely a figurehead, a symbol, and let Seward actually run the government. But Lincoln soon proved he was strong enough to corral these big egos. It wasn't long before Seward above all the rest became deeply devoted to Lincoln. He made it a point to tell friends that he and everyone else who had underestimated Lincoln's greatness had been profoundly mistaken. ❹

*Lincoln was such an unknown that his name was misspelled
on some campaign posters. His running mate,
Senator Hannibal Hamlin of Maine, was selected for him
by the delegates to the convention.*

1 2 3 4 5 6 7

8 9 → 10 ← 1 2 3

4 5 6 7 8 9 10 1 2

3 4 5 6 7 8 9 10 12

3 4 5 6 7 8 9 10

ONE TWO THREE FOUR FIVE SIX

DAY FIVE

APRIL 18,
1861

5

5

TREASON

Washington DC and
Charleston, South Carolina.

The Civil War started a few hours before dawn this morning. After decades of posturing and skirmishing by politicians, citizens, and bands of thugs, two armies have actually fired upon each other. In the four-month gap between Lincoln's election in November 1860, and his inauguration in March 1861, seven states have left the union. Instead of merely facing a local rebellion, the U.S. has been attacked by what some people claim to be a new nation, the Confederate States of America, which has been created to protect slave owners.

PALMETTO BUGS

The crisis began in October 1860, a full month before election day, when it was clear that Lincoln had a good chance of winning. The governor of South Carolina secretly invited the governors of other slave states to join in leaving—or "seceding from"—the Union. Most agreed to at least consider it. A few were enthusiastic. The governor of Florida replied that he was "proud to say that Florida will wheel into line with the gallant Palmetto State [South Carolina's nickname] or any other Cotton State or States. . . . If there is sufficient

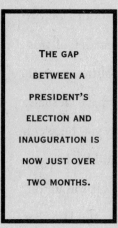

THE GAP
BETWEEN A
PRESIDENT'S
ELECTION AND
INAUGURATION IS
NOW JUST OVER
TWO MONTHS.

manliness at the South to strike for our rights, honor, and safety, in God's name let it be done before the inauguration of Lincoln."

For thirty years South Carolina had flirted seriously with secession, only to take a step back each time, largely because it might have found itself on its own. The anger reached full boil during the 1860 presidential election campaign. Politicians eager for the South to secede told voters Lincoln and his Republican Party were an immediate threat to the entire South. A lot of people were fooled. Many southerners believed Lincoln was determined to end slavery in the existing slave states. They believed he would give the full rights of citizenship to African Americans. They also believed he wanted to use force to impose his will on them. None of that was true. Although he hated slavery, Lincoln wasn't planning on giving African Americans the full rights of citizenship, such as the right to vote. (Nor was he planning to give those rights to women, who wouldn't gain them for another sixty years.) Had

Lincoln with his youngest son, Thomas, known to everyone as Tad. This photo was taken on February 1865, when Tad was not quite twelve years old. He and his older brother, Willie (opposite), were rarely disciplined by their parents, and they treated the White House as their own playground. When an invasion of Washington seemed likely at the beginning of the war, Tad and Willie built a play "fort" on the roof to defend the building. They had tutors instead of attending school, and Tad's education suffered as a result. It's possible his parents were indulgent because he had many health problems. He passed away just six years after his father's assassination, at age 18.

Willie Lincoln (above), was Tad's older brother by a bit more than three years. Although he was the older child in the White House, he was third of four Lincoln boys. The first, Edward, had passed away shortly before turning four. The second, Robert, was a student at Harvard University for most of his father's presidency.

Willie was more disciplined and thoughtful than Tad, but still able to get into trouble. Unfortunately, in February 1862, a little after this picture was taken, Willie died of what was probably typhoid fever. He was just over eleven years old. Both his parents were inconsolable. Some observers, including the president, believed Mrs. Lincoln's mental decline after Willie's death had signs of insanity.

the slave states accepted his one unwavering position, that slavery could not be extended into the western states, it's very possible that Lincoln would have defended the South against demands for the complete abolition of slavery.

Lincoln was frustrated that proslavery politicians were misrepresenting his positions. After his election, a pro-Union politician in the slave state of North Carolina asked him to make a public statement to calm the people of the South. Lincoln's reply was snippy, which was unusual. "May I be pardoned," he wrote, "if I ask whether even you have ever attempted to procure the reading of the Republican platform, or my speeches, by the Southern people? If not, what reason have I to expect that any additional production of mine would meet a better fate?"

The departing president, James Buchanan, made the crisis worse. At the beginning of December 1860, a month after Lincoln's election but before Buchanan left office, Buchanan attacked "the long continued and intemperate interference . . ." of the antislavery forces of the North, blaming them entirely for the conflict in his annual message to Congress. He did almost nothing to stop the southern states from seceding, and several members of his cabinet, sympathetic to the slave states, worked secretly to prevent the federal government from taking action.

Buchanan's defense of the South as it was preparing for secession and war has led many historians to rank him as the worst or among the worst American presidents. However, he did understand southern sentiment. He told Congress that the greatest motivation of the South was that the North's agitation had inspired the slaves "with vague notions of freedom. Hence a sense of security no longer exists around the family altar. This feeling of peace at home has given place to apprehensions of servile [slave] insurrections. Many a matron throughout the South retires at night in dread of what may befall herself and her children before the morning."

That fear was probably greatest of all in South Carolina, where slaves outnumbered free whites. Slaves were more than 57 percent of the state's population on the day the state seceded, December 20, 1860. (Adding the small number of free blacks, the total proportion of African Americans was nearly 59 percent.) Past attempts at uprisings had led South Carolina to enact laws preventing anyone from teaching a slave to read and write. Slaves weren't allowed to assemble in large numbers.

It's worth noting that the order in which the other states seceded is almost a perfect match for the relative sizes of their slave populations and white citizens. Mississippi, the state with the second-highest proportion of slaves to free white citizens (55 percent slaves), was the second state to leave the Union. The next four states to leave, Florida, Alabama, Georgia, and Louisiana, all had populations of about 45 percent slaves. Then came five states where slaves were between about 25 and 33 percent of the population.

DATES OF SECESSION AND SLAVE POPULATION

STATE	DATE OF SECESSION	SLAVES AS PERCENT OF TOTAL POPULATION
SOUTH CAROLINA	DEC. 20, 1860	57.20%
MISSISSIPPI	JAN. 9, 1861	55.20%
FLORIDA	JAN. 10, 1861	44.00%
ALABAMA	JAN. 11, 1861	45.10%
GEORGIA	JAN. 19, 1861	43.70%
LOUISIANA	JAN. 26, 1861	46.90%
TEXAS	FEB. 1, 1861	30.20%
VIRGINIA	APR. 17, 1861	30.80%
ARKANSAS	MAY 6, 1861	25.50%
TENNESSEE	MAY 6, 1861	24.90%
NORTH CAROLINA	MAY 20, 1861	33.40%

Source: U.S. Census Office, Eighth Census [1860], Population, Washington DC, 1864; and John C. Willis.

It's possible to look at these statistics and conclude that secession was about money. Slaves equalled property, and each slave had a dollar value. The states whose economies were most dependent on slaves were the first to leave the Union. But that's only part of the story. The fear of slave uprisings that President Buchanan mentioned also explains the order in which the southern states left. To a great extent, secession was the emotional reaction of a small ruling class who believed—possibly with very good reason—that they would soon lose power and be subject to the rule of people they had treated violently.

"HORNET'S NEST"

As the desire for war grew into a popular mania, Fort Sumter, sitting on an island in Charleston Harbor, became the focus of the warmongers' attention. Suddenly it became an insult to southerners for a United States fort to sit at the entrance of this important southern port. The federal commander was determined to defend it. While President Buchanan was still in office, the governor of South Carolina ordered a naval blockade to put the fort under siege. Buchanan tried to send relief, but the blockade turned away the federal ships.

When Lincoln took office at the beginning of March, 1861, he inherited this standoff. He recognized it as a test of his will. Although supplies were running low at the fort, the commander refused demands for surrender. To abandon the fort would be to signal his willingness to lose the South forever.

After about a month in office, Lincoln decided to try again to resupply the fort. He sent the governor of South Carolina a letter in advance, promising he was sending only basic supplies the men needed. He would not send ships or troops to break the blockade or attack the South Carolina forces.

The Confederate cabinet met to discuss Lincoln's

message. Instead of responding peacefully, they decided this was the moment to force the question of war. They would demand surrender of the fort, and if their demand was not met they would attack the fort and take it by force.

Some in the Confederate government knew this

SOUTH CAROLINA'S "ULTIMATUM."

A cartoon from early 1861, soon after the Fort Sumter crisis began. South Carolina governor Francis Pickens (left) is threatening President James Buchanan. He says, "Mr. President, if you don't surrender that fort at once, I'll be 'blowed' if I don't fire." Buchanan answers, "Oh don't! Governor Pickens, don't fire! till I get out of office." The cartoonist thinks the southern threat will backfire.

was a mistake. The Confederate secretary of state, Robert Toombs, who had been one of the most vocal supporters of secession, said the plan to take Sumter "is suicide, murder, and will lose us every friend at the North. You will wantonly strike a hornet's nest which extends from mountain to ocean, and legions now quiet will swarm out and sting us to death. . . . It is unnecessary; it puts us in the wrong; it is fatal."

He understood that the South would be at a great disadvantage in any war. It had half the population of the North—nine million to the North's twenty-two million. Factories capable of producing military equipment were mostly in the North. The business of the South was still very much to produce raw cotton that was then shipped to factories in the North or in the United Kingdom.

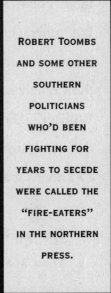

ROBERT TOOMBS AND SOME OTHER SOUTHERN POLITICIANS WHO'D BEEN FIGHTING FOR YEARS TO SECEDE WERE CALLED THE "FIRE-EATERS" IN THE NORTHERN PRESS.

Some southern politicians believed that if war began, a few important European countries, like the United Kingdom, would recognize the Confederacy and give it official status as a country. In return those countries would get valuable trading rights. But others in the South believed that the governments of Europe would be cautious. To recognize the Confederacy might lead to war with the Union. William T. Sherman, who would later become one of the most effective Union generals of the war, said to a southern friend:

> You people speak so lightly of war; you don't know what you're talking about. War is a terrible thing! . . . You mistake, too, the people of the North. They are a peaceable people but an earnest people. . . . They are not going to let this country be destroyed without a mighty effort to save it. The Northern people not only greatly outnumber the whites of the South, but . . . they

can make a steam engine, locomotive, or railway
car; hardly a yard of cloth or pair of shoes can
you make. . . . Only in your spirit and determi-
nation are you prepared for war. In all else you
are totally unprepared, with a bad cause to start
with. . .

If your people will but stop and think, they
must see in the end that you will surely fail.

In the end, however, the South was willing to fight a suicidal war to avoid living on equal terms with its slaves. Shortly after Alexander Stephens was sworn in as vice president of the Confederate States of America, he left no doubt about this essential difference in philosophy between the Confederacy and the U.S.:

The prevailing ideas entertained by [Thomas Jef-
ferson] and most of the leading statesmen at the
time of the formation of the old Constitution,
were that the enslavement of the African was in

violation of the laws of nature; that it was wrong
in principle, socially, morally, and politically. . . .
Our new government is founded upon exactly the
opposite idea; its foundations are laid, its corner-
stone rests upon the great truth, that the negro
is not equal to the white man; that slavery—
subordination to the superior race—is his natural
and normal condition. This, our new government,
is the first, in the history of the world, based upon
this great physical, philosophical, and moral
truth.

So now, on this day, not two months after taking office, Lincoln sees a telegram from the commander of the Union troops at Fort Sumter:

HAVING DEFENDED FORT SUMTER FOR THIRTY
FOUR HOURS UNTIL THE QUARTERS WERE
ENTIRELY BURNED THE MAIN GATES DESTROYED
BY FIRE, THE GORGE WALLS SERIOUSLY INJURED,

THE MAGAZINE SURROUNDED BY FLAMES AND ITS DOOR CLOSED FROM THE EFFECTS OF HEAT, FOUR BARRELS AND THREE CARTRIDGES OF POWDER ONLY BEING AVAILABLE AND NO PROVISIONS REMAINING BUT PORK, I ACCEPTED TERMS OF EVACUATION . . . ROBERT ANDERSON. MAJOR FIRST ARTILLERY. COMMANDING.

This is the event that will shock the North, rally the South, and begin a conflict that will settle the slavery question. **5**

The rebel bombardment of Fort Sumter

DEFEAT

Washington DC.

In the telegraph office of the War Department building, just a few steps across the White House lawn from Lincoln's office, the telegraph operators keep their hands hard over their earpieces to block out the noise of the men crowding the room. Lincoln's staff and army officers have maps spread out on tables, and are trying to picture the movements of troops as they're being reported over the wires.

The dispatches are from a field telegraph office a few miles from the fighting, in the first true battle of the war. Fresh Union volunteers and equally inexperienced Confederate soldiers are on a battlefield about thirty miles southwest of Washington, near Manassas, Virginia.

IN THE SOUTH, THIS ENCOUNTER WAS CALLED THE BATTLE OF MANASSAS. IN THE NORTH, IT WAS CALLED THE BATTLE OF BULL RUN. (LATER, WHEN A SECOND BATTLE WAS FOUGHT IN THE SAME PLACE, THIS ONE BECAME KNOWN AS THE FIRST BATTLE OF BULL RUN AND THE FIRST BATTLE OF MANASSAS.) HISTORIANS STILL TEND TO USE THE NAME DISTINCTIVE TO THEIR REGIONS.

So far, the news coming to the War Department is very good. The mood of the day, described by one observer as "feverish excitement and little, if any, alarm," is becoming more relaxed. No one is ready to celebrate yet, but there's a feeling of confidence on the part of Lincoln and his staff that the many predictions of a quick Union victory and an end to the southern rebellion will prove true today.

"THE WHOLE NORTH AROSE"

I t has been three months since South Carolina attacked Fort Sumter. The country looks nothing like it did when Lincoln took office a little bit before then.

Immediately after the fall of Fort Sumter, Lincoln telegraphed the governors of all the states asking for volunteers to join the army and put down the rebellion. That was a moment of decision for most of the states in the Union.

Beriah Magoffin, governor of Kentucky, replied to Lincoln: "I say emphatically Kentucky will furnish no troops for the wicked purpose of subduing her sister's southern states." John W. Ellis, governor of North Carolina, wrote, "I regard the levy of troops made by the administration for the purpose of subjugating the states of the South as in violation of the Constitution and the gross usurpation of power. I can be no party to this wicked violation of the laws of the country and to this war upon the liberties of the free people. You can get no troops from North Carolina." The governor of Tennessee, Isham G. Harris, wrote: "Tennessee will not furnish a single man for purpose of concord should, but 50,000, if necessary, for the defense of our rights and those of our southern brethren." Claiborne Fox Jackson, governor of Missouri, wrote: "your requisition, in my judgment, is illegal, unconstitutional, and revolutionary in its object, inhuman and diabolical, and cannot be complied with. Not one man will the state of Missouri furnish to carry on any such unholy crusade." Instead, these governors offered troops to the Confederate Army. Lincoln was disappointed but not surprised.

In the North, however, the response was just as strong in support of the Union. First came shock. In the North, the threat of attack on Fort Sumter had been considered "the idle bluster of angry disappointment," as one Boston eyewitness put it. The fort's surrender "fell on the land like a thunderbolt." But in response to Lincoln's request for volunteers, "the whole North arose as one man."

What Lincoln needed most urgently was protection for Washington DC. The nation's capital sits right on the borders of Virginia and Maryland, two dangerous states at the time. Virginia, which seceded just two days after Lincoln asked for troops, was one of the most powerful states in the Confederacy. Maryland, also a slave state, had not yet seceded, but its sympathies were with the Confederacy. When the first northern troops headed for Washington reached Baltimore, Maryland, about forty miles north of their destination, a mob attacked them. The mayor of Baltimore told Lincoln, "It is not possible for more soldiers to pass through Baltimore unless they fight their way at every step." The troops had to get off their trains and march a different route to Washington. Lincoln, like every other Union supporter in the city, had to wait anxiously for several days, during which the capital was open to an invasion from nearby rebel soldiers in Virginia. Rebel sympathizers in Maryland had cut the telegraph lines to the capital and blocked the railways, so the city was truly on its own. Fortunately, the Union troops arrived before any attack was attempted.

> THE CONFEDERACY'S CAPITAL FOR MOST OF ITS EXISTENCE WAS RICHMOND, VIRGINIA, JUST ONE HUNDRED MILES SOUTH OF WASHINGTON DC.

But that first crisis was soon replaced with others. Arkansas, Tennessee, and North Carolina joined the rebellion. On the day of this first battle, eleven former Union states now call themselves the Confederate States of America. The country is truly divided.

THE FAST AND THE FURIOUS

As each state seceded, many of the soldiers and sailors from those states switched their allegiance to the South. These included important officers. Lincoln had to reorganize the Union's army and navy before the rebellion could be stopped.

The seventy-five thousand volunteers who joined the cause after Lincoln's request for troops had signed up for just one hundred days. Some officers felt that was barely enough time to train the new recruits. But other aides, as well as influential journalists, shared the public's general opinion that a swift, overwhelming action by the North would lead to immediate victory. The self-puffery that had led the South to attack Fort Sumter was present in the North, too. Overconfidence and wishful thinking about a single decisive battle are common mistakes in warfare.

Lincoln gave his commanders as much time as he could, but it was impossible to ignore the hundred-day deadline after which his soldiers would return home. Shortly before the deadline, he ordered his generals to bring the fight to the rebels in Virginia.

eading up to the battle, confidence in the North was so high that journalists and citizens made plans for picnics near the front to watch the fighting. Now that the battle has begun, the reports telegraphed back to the War Department in Washington every fifteen minutes confirm that Union troops are advancing easily. The field officers say the battle is essentially over.

Then something seems to go wrong. A confusing telegram arrives from an army captain: "The day is lost. . . . The routed troops will not re-form." The message warns that Washington is in danger.

No one can find Lincoln. After the positive early dispatches, he had gone for an evening drive. Meanwhile, more messages are arriving that confirm a sudden turn of events: As soon as the Union troops completed their advance toward the Confederate positions, the Confederates began a counterattack.

The chaos begins at Bull Run. The American flag is on the ground and the Union soldier near it is running away from the battle.

Lincoln gets the news when he returns to the White House. He walks calmly but quickly to the telegraph office. Everyone is staring so closely at maps of the battlefield that at first they don't notice he has arrived. Soon more reports come over the wire: Facing the Confederate cannons and tough resistance from Confederate troops, the Union soldiers have turned and run.

The men in the room look to Lincoln for a reaction. His expression is grim, but he's not frightened. Many people are less steadfast. The poet Walt Whitman later wrote, "In Washington, among the great persons and their entourage, [there is] a mixture of awful consternation, uncertainty, rage, shame, helplessness, and stupefying disappointment. The worst is not only imminent, but already here. . . ."

All night, Lincoln receives visitors at the White House who witnessed the scene. He learns that the road along which the Union troops made their orderly advance became chaotic. Troops threw their heavy equipment off to the side so they could retreat more quickly. Drivers of equipment wagons, finding that their horses couldn't make it through the mob on the road, simply abandoned their wagons and horses and joined the soldiers retreating on foot. Cannons, ammunition, thousand of rifles, and other equipment littered the battlefield and the roadside.

Similar reports spread panic throughout Washington.

Whitman would say that, "the talk among certain of the magnates and officers and clerks and officials everywhere . . . was loud and undisguised for yielding out and out, and substituting the southern rule, and Lincoln promptly abdicating and departing."

Lincoln doesn't waver. Through the night, he makes further plans for the army based on what he has learned from this battle. "If there were nothing else of Abraham Lincoln for history to stamp him with," Whitman concluded, "it is enough . . . that he endured that hour, that day . . . —indeed a crucifixion day—that it did not conquer him—that he unflinchingly stemm'd it, and resolv'd to lift himself and the Union out of it."

The battle had proved the two sides were equally matched in many ways. They had similar weapons, similar training, and a similar familiarity with the terrain. On any given day, either might win. That meant this war would be decided by the ability to take a blow and still move forward. In this regard, as

William T. Sherman had written to his friend around the time of the attack on Fort Sumter, the North had all the advantages: more men, more factories to produce weapons, and a government with more money to support the war effort. The idea that a swift attack would break the other side's will to fight was as foolish on this day as it had been when Fort Sumter was taken. The bloodiest war in history has now formally begun. **6**

At left is Simon Cameron, Lincoln's first Secretary of War. He had been promised a cabinet position by Lincoln's aides in return for staying out of the convention battle that led to Lincoln's nomination. Unfortunately, he was deeply corrupt, and not a competent manager of the War Department. He was forced to resign in 1862.

Lincoln then gave the post to one of Cameron's chief aides, Edwin Stanton (right). Stanton, who had been attorney general during the pro-slavery presidency of James Buchanan, seemed an odd choice at first, but his commitment to the preservation of the Union and his effectiveness as a manager was unquestionable. He and Lincoln had very different styles—Stanton had almost no sense of humor, while Lincoln interrupted the most serious discussions if a joke came to mind—yet they grew to have great respect for each other. In time, Stanton also came to share many of Lincoln's political views.

DAY 7

SEVEN

ONE TWO THREE FOUR FIVE SIX

SEPTEMBER 22, 1862

EMANCIPATION

Washington DC.

For the Union, the war has not been going well. Most of Lincoln's generals have been a disappointment. After battles at Bull Run and Shiloh, where Confederate forces scored heavily, feelings of doubt about the wisdom of the war are already being expressed in the North.

At the same time, Lincoln is moving steadily toward a huge political risk that could be a greater disaster than any single battle. While the rest of his party debates if, when, and how to end slavery, he has decided to do it himself now. That decision could split the country again and drive more states into the Confederacy.

BORDERLINE PERSONALITIES

Lincoln has already tried many times to end slavery, and thus end the war, by offering money to slave owners. He has been tiptoeing around this explosive issue because he doesn't want Delaware, Maryland, Kentucky, Missouri, and West Virginia—the Union slave states known as the "border states" because they border the Confederacy—to switch sides.

If he loses the border states, the North will probably lose the war. Washington DC, which is surrounded by Maryland and Virginia, would immediately be cut off from the rest of the Union. Even one state can make a difference. "I think to lose Kentucky is nearly the same as to lose the whole game," Lincoln has said. If that state were to switch, others would probably follow, and the South would also gain a route to northern cities near the Great Lakes.

The governments and large numbers of the citizens of the border states are highly sensitive to any move by Lincoln that interferes with what they believe to be their rights, especially with regard to slavery.

Lincoln already spends a lot of time trying to keep the border states happy. It isn't easy. When one of his generals announced a military order declaring emancipation for all the slaves in the Confederate states of Georgia, South Carolina, and Florida, Lincoln overturned the order to avoid angering the border states.

A few months before this day, he invited senators and representatives from the border states to the White House to urge them to accept his latest offer to buy the freedom of slaves. In a firm voice, he rebuked their failure to support his earlier offers. "You of the border states hold more power for good than any other equal number of members," he told them. "If you all had voted for [his proposal to buy the slaves' freedom] in the gradual emancipation message of last March, the war would now be substantially ended." As long as the border states allow slavery, he reminds them, the South will believe they'll switch sides and join the fight against the Union. That hope is keeping the South in the fight. "By conceding what I now ask, you can relieve me, and much more, can relieve the country." Knowing that they fear living among free African Americans, he promises them that they do not have to free all the slaves at once, and he will make it easy for freed slaves to resettle in other countries. But the border state politicians are no more interested than before.

That's when Lincoln knew he had to act alone.

The war itself seems to have changed Lincoln's attitude toward the presidency. He believed Congress was principally responsible for actions affecting the public. Now he sees too many decisions that must be made by the country's chief executive, rather than its elected representatives. When the war began, Lincoln was more likely to defer to the opinions of his advisers and generals, but he has learned that the reputations of some exceed their abilities. Lincoln has now begun to take more direct control of military operations. This decision about slavery, he concludes, is simply an extension of the country's military efforts, not a Constitutional battle between state and federal governments.

He has prepared carefully for this moment. The month before, while waiting at the telegraph office for news of the latest battles, Lincoln began to make notes for an emancipation order. The superintendent of the office, to whom he gave the pad of paper each night for safekeeping, later remembered, "He would look out of the window a while and then put his pen to paper, but he did not write much at once. He would study between times and when he had made up his mind he would put down a line or two, and then sit quiet for a few minutes. After a time he would resume his writing, only to stop again at intervals to make some remark to me or to one of the cipher operators as a fresh dispatch from the front was handed to him. . . . this he did nearly every day for several weeks. . . . Sometimes he would not write more than a line or two, and once I observed that he put question marks on the margin of what he'd written."

Soon after the document was finished, at an earlier meeting of his cabinet, Lincoln revealed his plan. Secretary of the Treasury Chase, the most avid abolitionist, asked for stronger language about bringing freed slaves into the army. Montgomery Blair, the postmaster general, who was more moderate, worried that the proclamation would cost the Republican Party seats in the upcoming congressional elections. But it was Secretary of State Seward who made the most interesting point. "I approve of the proclamation," he said, but "the depression of the public mind" after so many losses on the battlefield may make it look like "the last measure of an exhausted government, a cry for help [from the government to the slave popula-tion]." Seward suggesting postponing it until after a better result in the battlefield. Lincoln later said that, "the wisdom of the view of the Secretary of State struck me with very great force. It was an aspect of the case that, in all my thought upon the subject, I had entirely overlooked. The result was that I put the draft of the proclamation aside . . . waiting for a victory."

That victory—or something close enough to one—came at the Battle of Antietam, just a few days before this day's cabinet meeting. In a single day of fighting that saw 23,000 soldiers from both sides wounded or killed, the Union Army stopped a Confederate invasion of Maryland. Although Union General George McClellan failed to pursue Robert E. Lee's army and possibly finish the war, the North considered it a win for its side. Lincoln had his opening for the Emancipation Proclamation.

"THE TIME HAS COME"

n this day, he has called a special cabinet meeting for noon. The members, some who once considered him little more than a backwoods lawyer, and inadequate to the job of president, now hear the words of a confident leader:

"Several weeks ago, I read to you an order I had prepared," he reminds them, "which, on account of objections made by some of you, was not issued. I think the time has come now."

Before anyone can voice an objection, Lincoln

makes clear he is not interested in any further discussion about whether or not the document should be released. He is only open to suggestions that improve it. There is a steely edge to his words. Others might say it better, he acknowledges, but "there is no way in which I can have any other man put where I am. I am here. I must do the best I can, and bear the responsibility of taking the course which I feel I ought to take."

With that, he orders the public announcement of his Emancipation Proclamation.

The terms of the proclamation are complicated.

Lincoln announces the proclamation to his cabinet (left to right): Edwin Stanton, Salmon Chase, Gideon Welles, Caleb Smith, William Seward (seated), Montgomery Blair, and Edward Bates.

It does not simply free all slaves throughout the Union and the Confederacy. Instead, it once again extends an offer of compensation, but declares that any state that persists in rebelling when the new year begins on January 1, 1863, will lose any protections it might have under the Constitution, including slavery rights. Ironically, this means that the Emancipation Proclamation does not free the slaves in the Union's own slave states. For that reason, its usefulness has often been questioned. But most reasonable historians conclude this truly is a crucial moment in the war. The Emancipation Proclamation is the first step toward establishing the new basis on which the country will exist when the war ends. The war won't merely stop the western expansion of slavery; it will abolish the institution altogether.

The proclamation will also clarify the North's relations with foreign countries. The United Kingdom and France, for example, still profit from business ties with the South, and the continued economic support of the United Kingdom especially is crucial to the Confederacy. But these nations have both abolished slavery—the United Kingdom much more recently—so when the war becomes not merely a legal crisis between two slave nations but an effort to end slavery in both the Union and the Confederacy, popular support from the United Kingdom and France will swing immediately to the North. This will lead to serious financial problems for the Confederacy, which needs European money to continue the fight.

In the North itself, many people, perhaps even most, will welcome the proclamation. They've been fighting to end slavery all along. Others, however, will fear that freed slaves will move north and take their jobs.

But as the magazine *Harper's Weekly* admitted when it considered the question of the proclamation, even though "at the present time a moral antipathy for the Negro is entertained by a large class of persons at the North," the war was leading to a "remarkable change" among many people. Soldiers in the field "who, a year ago, really believed, that slavery was the true station for the Negro," now, after seeing the conditions of slavery firsthand, and living among African Americans, "freely expressed what used to be called 'abolition views.'" The real question, the editors suggested, was "how long it will take for these liberal views to permeate society, and stamp themselves on the mind of the working class...." Unfortunately, that question could still be asked more than a century after the Emancipation Proclamation. But this day marks one giant step forward. **7**

Lincoln meets with General George McClellan in the general's tent headquarters at Antietam, Maryland, in October 1862. Admired for his ability to train soldiers, McClellan had risen far above his ability to command. But he imagined himself the most capable man of his generation, and constantly blamed others for his failures. His disrepectful attitude toward Lincoln, his commander-in-chief, had been apparent from the moment he took command of the army. He sometimes refused to meet with the president, and even ignored Lincoln when the president took the trouble to find him. At the time of the meeting pictured here, the battle had already taken place. McClellan was unwilling to follow Lincoln's orders to pursue the retreating Confederate forces, an action that might have ended the war. About a month later, long after McClellan had lost the confidence of Lincoln's colleagues, Lincoln fired him.

"SHALL NOT PERISH"

Gettysburg, Pennsylvania.

n a horse that's a bit too small for his great height, Abraham Lincoln slowly rides toward Gettysburg's Cemetery Hill, trailed by an entourage that includes several governors, dozens of army officers and members of Congress, and a few of his cabinet officers. A few months earlier on the same spot, Union and Confederate armies fought for three days, leaving the largest number of casualties of any battle during the war. Thirty thousand men were wounded, and seven thousand dead men are scattered through the fields in and around Gettysburg. Simply burying that many dead was a difficult task. To prevent the rotting corpses from spreading disease, many of the men were buried in shallow graves where they had fallen. But some of the townspeople of Gettysburg are determined that those soldiers should have a more fitting memorial, and on this day an area of the hill near the old town cemetery is being dedicated to the Union war dead. (The soldiers who fought for the Confederacy were left in their original graves until a few years after the war ended.)

EYES ON THE PRIZE

The Battle of Gettysburg, which took place from July 1 through July 3, 1863, is often called a turning point in the war. Up to that point, the armies of the Confederacy had been winning most of the important battles, especially in the east, near Washington DC. Robert E. Lee, in command of the rebel Army of Northern Virginia, decided to invade the North, marching his eighty thousand men across the border into Maryland and then into southern Pennsylvania. He hoped that by bringing the fighting to the North, he could lead politicians there to give up the war. When he met the Union Army at Gettysburg, an even greater prize seemed possible: defeat of the Union Army would leave Washington—less than eighty miles to the south—under-defended. But the Union army held its ground, and by the third day Lee's defeated forces were retreating as quickly as they could.

Had the Union commander, General George Meade, advanced on Lee's retreating army, he might have finished the Confederacy. But not only did he fail to advance quickly at the end of the battle, he ignored an opportunity when Lee's army was trapped on the banks of the flooding Potomac River, which was impossible to cross. Perhaps he was unsure of himself, having gained command of the Union troops just three days before the battle, when he replaced another general. Lincoln, who knew that Gettysburg could have meant the end of the war rather than just a turning point, was disappointed.

Part of the audience at Gettysburg

Reaching the cemetery site, Lincoln steps onto the raised wooden platform, about four or five feet high, that has been built for the occasion. A flag has been draped across the front of the platform. Ten thousand people, maybe more, have gathered for the ceremony.

After Lincoln settles into a chair in the front row on the stage, Edward Everett, the most popular public speaker of the day, begins a two-hour performance, all of it from memory, describing the great battle that took place four and a half months earlier. It's a speech that he has written and even published weeks before the event, but Lincoln, who was sent a copy and is prepared for its length, does his best to look attentive.

Lincoln has been drafting and revising his remarks for a few weeks, but they remain, as he has told one friend, "short, short, short." Various people on the trip have seen him making revisions on the train ride to Gettysburg. He was still making changes just before going to bed the evening before the speech. As Everett's long performance continues, Lincoln takes the speech out of his pocket and looks at it once again, almost as if he were ready to revise it on the spot. But he puts it back in his pocket and waits patiently. About Everett's speech, a reporter later said, "So cold! If only it were alive!" Finally, Everett finishes. The crowd seems more exhausted than excited.

Now Lincoln stands. As a young eyewitness later put it, the "flutter and motion of the crowd ceased the moment the president was on his feet. Such was the quiet that his footfalls, I remember very distinctly, woke echoes, and with the creaking of the boards, it was as if some one were walking through the hall-ways of an empty house." In a sense, that's exactly what Lincoln has been doing for years. Despite being the man at the center of one of the largest conflicts in the history of the world, he remains, as he has felt for much of his life, alone with his thoughts. He knows that the dead men being honored went into battle on his orders. He knows that the war might have ended before the Battle of Gettysburg if it had been better directed. He also knows that many of the soldiers who died felt a great personal loyalty to him, even if they did not agree with all of the reasons for the war.

He has spent so much time on these "short, short, short" remarks because he wants to honor the war dead with an honest statement about the cause for which they died. For Lincoln, it comes down to the same few words that have been his guiding light since he was a child: "all men are created equal." Ending slavery was one part of living up to that ideal, but there was something else: The war was also a test of democracy. It had been less than a hundred years since American independence, and self-government was still rare in the world. Europe was still ruled by monarchies. Many people still considered the United States to be an experiment rather than a lasting nation—an experiment that would probably fail.

Lincoln puts on his glasses and begins to express his simple, powerful beliefs. "Four score and seven years ago our fathers brought forth on this continent a new nation, conceived in Liberty, and dedicated to the proposition that all men are created equal. Now we are engaged in a great civil war, testing whether that nation, or any nation, so conceived and so dedicated, can long endure." The Civil War has gone beyond a battle for freedom and equality for slaves. It's become a test of the principle of equality for all Americans, who have claimed the right to self-government and now must govern themselves wisely. Early in the war, Lincoln said to his personal secretary,

HISTORIAN JAMES MCPHERSON HAS OBSERVED THAT EARLY IN LINCOLN'S PRESIDENCY, LINCOLN USUALLY REFERS TO THE UNITED STATES AS A "UNION"— SUGGESTING A COLLECTION OF NEARLY-INDEPENDENT GOVERNMENTS— BUT IN THE GETTYSBURG ADDRESS, LINCOLN CONTINUALLY REFERS TO THE COUNTRY AS A SINGLE "NATION."

*In the background of this photo from the ceremony, officials in tall
formal hats and others wearing sashes across their chests can be
seen on the podium that elevates them slightly above the audience.
The figure in the circle has recently been identified as Lincoln.
He's in a chair in the front row of the podium, and seems to be
looking at his lap, possibly reviewing his speech.*

John Hay, "The central idea pervading this struggle is
the necessity that is upon us, of proving that popular
government is not an absurdity. . . . If we fail it will go
far to prove the incapability of the people to govern

themselves." That is what he tells the crowd this day: They must dedicate themselves to the idea for which so many lives were lost, so that "government of the people, by the people, for the people, shall not perish from the earth."

For a moment, the crowd is silent. After Everett's long speech, they don't believe the president is really finished after fewer than three hundred words. Even when he returns to his seat, a young reporter, who expected much more, asks Lincoln, "Is that all?"

"Yes, for the present," Lincoln answers.

Ironically, Edward Everett is one of the few who immediately sees the speech's brilliance. He later sends the president a short note: "I should be glad if I could flatter myself that I came as near to the central idea of the occasion in two hours as you did in two minutes." **8**

THE GETTYSBURG ADDRESS

Four score and seven years ago our fathers brought forth, upon this continent, a new nation, conceived in liberty, and dedicated to the proposition that "all men are created equal."

Now we are engaged in a great civil war, testing whether that nation, or any nation so conceived, and so dedicated, can long endure. We are met on a great battle field of that war. We have come to dedicate a portion of it, as a final resting place for those who died here, that the nation might live. This we may, in all propriety do. But, in a larger sense, we can not dedicate—we can not consecrate—we can not hallow, this ground—The brave men, living and dead, who struggled here, have hallowed it, far above our poor power to add or detract. The world will little note, nor long remember what we say here; while it can never forget what they did here.

It is rather for us, the living, we here be dedicated to the great task remaining before us—that, from these honored dead we take increased devotion to that cause for which they here, gave the last full measure of devotion—that we here highly resolve these dead shall not have died in vain; that the nation, shall have a new birth of freedom, and that government of the people by the people for the people, shall not perish from the earth.

This text is from what's known as the "Nicolay" version of the speech, one of a few that exist. It may be closest to what Lincoln read at the ceremony, though later revisions are often taught.

VICTORY

Washington DC and Appomattox, Virginia.

As the steamboat *River Queen* chugs toward the Washington Navy Yard, its distinguished passengers stand at the deck rail and watch the capital come into view. The city is glowing with the light of hundreds of bonfires. Cheering and shouting and singing is heard from the streets.

On the boat, Lincoln, his face lit by the warm orange light, is smiling. For two weeks he has been away from the minute-to-minute worries of the

White House, on a trip to the war front in Virginia. Although he has seen the deadly results of some battles there, he's also witnessed the advance of the Union Army, and knows victory is close. His aides have noticed that his mood, often so grim during the last four years, has relaxed. His "indescribable sadness," said one friend, has been replaced by an expression of "serene joy."

The citizens of Washington are celebrating the capture of the Confederate capital of Richmond, Virginia, just six days earlier. After hearing news of the victory, Lincoln rushed to Richmond and walked directly to the mansion that Jefferson Davis, the president of the Confederacy, had recently fled. Entering Davis's former office, Lincoln "sank down in" the chair, according to one of his aides. The war was not yet completely over, but it was as if the chess game had been won. King had captured king.

Before returning to the White House, Lincoln

stops to visit Secretary of State Seward, who had been badly injured in a carriage accident a few days before. "I think we are near the end, at last," he reassures his friend. But Seward's injury has left Lincoln worried. Back at the White House his old sadness seems to have returned.

Then, as he's catching up on a few things before heading for bed, he's interrupted by his secretary of war. Edwin Stanton is carrying a telegram just received from the head of the Union Army, General Ulysses S. Grant: "General Lee surrendered the Army of Northern Virginia this afternoon on terms proposed by myself."

Although Lee's men account for only about one-sixth of the total Confederate forces, Lee's stature, and the strategic importance of his army, means the war should be over in days rather than months. It's simply a question of how long the remaining rebels resist the inevitable.

More telegrams arrive with details of Lee's surrender. After the fall of Richmond, Grant guessed correctly that Lee would head toward the railway at Appomattox Station. The Union Army got there first, cutting off the rebels' supplies and any chance of escape. Lee, who had already refused one request by Grant to surrender, now ignored another. But Lee's aides finally convinced their commander that it was useless to fight further. The usual formal notes were exchanged, and a meeting of the two generals was set for the Appomattox Court House.

Lee arrived in full splendor: a new uniform, clean boots, and a glittering sword. Grant, as usual, wore a simple, old shirt, unbuttoned to reveal his undershirt, and worn, muddy boots. Although he hadn't changed into ceremonial dress, Grant showed deep respect for his rival, who in fact had been the most admired soldier in the U.S. Army before choosing to fight for the Confederacy. He also offered Lee generous surrender terms: Lee's men merely give up their army weapons and give their word that they would not fight again. They could immediately return home with whatever possessions they owned. These terms were in keeping with the desires of Lincoln. He had told Grant he wanted to let the rebel soldiers get back to work on their farms and in their stores.

After the surrender papers were signed, Grant and

Lee and Grant, surrounded by aides, at the surrender talks

Lee shook hands, and Lee excused himself. While he waited on the porch of the courthouse for his horse, his frustration finally broke through his stiff formality. Union officers saw the famous Confederate general punch the palm of his left hand with his right fist three times.

ALL'S FAIR IN LOVE AND WAR

Eighteen months earlier, few people would have guessed that Lee would consider surrender, and fewer still would have guessed it would be to Grant. Lee and his army had escaped at Gettysburg. The Union Army seemed to miss every chance it had to defeat the Confederates. When Union General Meade failed to finish Lee at Gettysburg, Lincoln gave greater responsibility to Grant, who had been winning important battles in the West. Lincoln admired Grant's fighting spirit. In March of

1864, Grant was put in command of the entire Union Army. He immediately devised a strategy to attack the Confederate forces in several places at once, and to destroy whatever civilian property and businesses were being used to support the Confederacy. This was a change from the military etiquette of the time, which called for armies only to fight other armies. Grant didn't care. He wanted the war to end, and wasn't worried about being called impolite. His determination, however, caused his reputation to suffer. Under his command, the armies fought more, and that meant more casualties. He was unfairly accused of not caring about the deaths. He also refused prisoner exchanges with the South, because he knew that he could replace a Union soldier being held by the Confederacy more easily than the Confederacy could replace one of the soldiers he was holding. Families of imprisoned Union soldiers hated Grant for this policy, but Lincoln supported him. The two men usually thought alike, and the respect that each felt for the other was a relief to

Ulysses S. Grant (1822–1885) graduated from West Point and served with distinction in the Mexican-American War but failed to advance as an officer and left the army. He rejoined when the Civil War began. As a result of his great military successes, he was elected president in 1868. Unfortunately, his experience in the field hadn't prepared him for politics. Honest himself, and overly trusting of others, his administration became a favorite of corrupt politicians and their associates.

Lincoln after so many disappointing generals during the first two years of the war.

THE WAR AT HOME

L incoln had his own battles. To pay for the war, he needed money from Congress, and to get the approval of congressmen, he often had to offer favors in return, such as political and military jobs. His cabinet members continued to battle with one another, sometimes because of real philosophical differences, other times merely because their personalities clashed. As the election of 1864 approached, one member of the cabinet, Secretary of the Treasury Chase, tried to take the Republican Party nomination from Lincoln. While that effort came to nothing, Lincoln's Democratic opponent was almost as surprising: General George McClellan, formerly commander of the Union army, whose enormous vanity and utter lack of fighting ability had frustrated Lincoln at the beginning of the war and allowed the rebels a long string of victories. McClellan promised to negotiate peace with the Confederacy to end the war.

A lot of Americans liked the idea of a peace settlement. Many northern laborers were fearful that a flood of freed slaves would take their jobs. Some hated the idea of risking their lives for people they imagined to be an economic threat. There had been riots

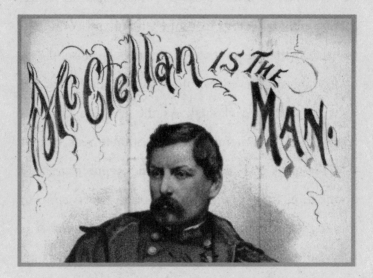

The cover page of a campaign song from the 1864 election

when Lincoln ordered young men into military service. Some Americans were simply exhausted by the war. The casualties were far beyond what anyone had imagined they'd be when war began. In the early days of 1864, before Grant took full command of the army, there were few victories to strengthen voters' confidence.

But under Grant and generals like William T. Sherman, the Union army moved steadily forward as election day approached. Important victories, like the capture of Atlanta, Georgia, changed the public's mood. In the election, Lincoln won a majority of votes, and in the electoral college beat McClellan 212 votes to 21 votes. (Andrew Johnson, from the rival Democratic Party, ran as Lincoln's vice president. The old rival parties joined for this one election in what was called the National Union Party.)

Lincoln has already dedicated his second term as president to the cause of Reconstruction, the rebuilding of the nation after the war's inevitable end. Many in his party want the South to be punished. Lincoln, as he has said publicly, and as he has more recently instructed Grant, feels differently. In his Second Inaugural Address, he asked that the country proceed "with malice toward none" and "charity for all," to achieve "a just and a lasting peace."

THEY'RE PLAYING OUR SONG

rom a window in the White House, Lincoln looks out at the street celebrations. He knows the partying will last all week. This morning's surrender by Lee comes just a few days before the fourth anniversary of South Carolina's bombardment of Fort Sumter, which started the war. Fort Sumter is also back in Union hands, and official celebrations have already been planned to mark the anniversary.

Although he had hoped to watch unnoticed,

someone on the street spots him in the window, and soon a crowd is outside the White House, serenading him. The crowd is shouting for him to make a speech. "I suppose arrangements are being made for some sort of formal demonstration, this, or perhaps, tomorrow night," he says. "I shall have nothing to say if you dribble it all out of me before!"

"We can't wait!" the crowd calls back.

"Well," Lincoln says, "I see you have a band with you."

"We have two or three!"

"Well then, I've always thought 'Dixie' one of the best tunes I've ever heard. Our adversaries over the way attempted to appropriate it, but I insisted yesterday that we fairly captured it."

The crowd interrupts him with a cheer.

"I presented the question to the Attorney General," Lincoln continues, "and he gave it as his legal opinion that it is our lawful prize. I now request the band to favor me with its performance!" ❾

ONE TWO THREE FOUR FIVE SIX

DAY 10

APRIL 14,
1865

TEN

ASSASSINATION

Washington DC, 8:00 A.M.

A braham Lincoln is already at his messy desk. As usual, the War Office delivered a stack of fresh telegrams during the night. Reading them is how he begins each day. He's expecting good news. He flips through the telegrams to see if anything has arrived from General Sherman, whose troops are rushing to capture the important Confederate seaport of Savannah, Georgia. After Lee's surrender to Grant at Appomattox a few days ago, and the fall of Richmond, the Confederate capital, a week before that, a victory by Sherman would mean the end of fighting. Lincoln has no doubt the war will end without another large battle.

The news about Lee and Richmond has put Washington in a good mood. Because the city is located right on the edge of the Confederacy, it's been under threat of invasion since the war began. Residents, exhausted by the tension, are now giddy. Celebrations began soon after the news about Lee was announced five days earlier. The troops guarding the city fired their cannons in salute. Happy crowds have been outside the White House since the news broke.

But the celebrations have made one man nervous. Colonel William H. Crook, the Lincoln's main body-guard, arrives to begin his shift. As usual, he starts the day by checking that a guard is present outside the president's office door. Then, in a change from routine, he steps outside to keep watch on the drunken crowd in the nearby streets. Even though it's early morning, the celebration continues. Later he would admit to a worry: "Those about the President lost somewhat of the feeling, usually present, that his life was not safe." Because the war was essentially over, they were less careful about the president's safety. But he will be off duty this evening when the Lincolns attend a show at Ford's Theatre. A backup will have to take his place.

ALL THE WORLD'S A STAGE

In a hotel just ten blocks from the White House, John Wilkes Booth, proud of his handsome looks, combs a scented, greasy wax through his curly hair. He's an actor, from a famous theater family, and it shows in his dramatic flair. His clothes are expensive and immaculate. His boots are shined, as always. His imagination is just as dramatic. He believes he can save the Confederacy. A few weeks ago, he'd

John Wilkes Booth (1838–1865). His father Junius and his older brother Edwin were the leading American actors of their generations. To a lesser degree, John's acting career was also successful. Although often called a madman, his hatred of Lincoln came from not from insanity but from his extreme political beliefs. He supported slavery and disapproved of Lincoln's efforts to stop the Southern rebellion.

made serious plans to kidnap Lincoln, hoping to trade the president for Confederate prisoners of war who could then resume fighting. Now that Robert E. Lee has surrendered part of the Confederate Army, Booth is even more desperate. In a few hours, he'll impulsively decide to commit an act that he believes will make him a hero, a guardian of liberty: kill Lincoln.

Shortly before noon, when he goes to Ford's Theatre to pick up his mail, Booth learns Lincoln plans to attend this evening's performance of a popular comedy, *Our American Cousin*. Booth immediately realizes this may be his best chance. As a well-known actor, he's familiar to the theater staff, who won't question him if he's wandering around the building. He knows how to get to Lincoln's private box. He's also familiar with the play that's on this evening, so he'll know at exactly when to strike and how to escape.

It's a bold plan, but that's not all of it. He meets with his accomplices from the kidnapping scheme and they add other targets. One accomplice will kill Vice President Andrew Johnson at the same time Booth is killing Lincoln. Another will kill Secretary of State Seward. Booth hopes to plunge the U.S. government into chaos, giving the Confederacy one more chance to survive.

THE REMAINS OF THE DAY

While the conspirators are plotting, the president is meeting with his cabinet. Lincoln reminds the men that he believes the country's divisions must be healed through compassion, not vengeance. Thus there must be no persecutions, he says, no "hanging or killing these [rebel] men, even the worst of them." Lincoln and the cabinet also talk about the future of the freed slaves. Where will they go? How will they survive? Should they be allowed to vote? The questions are debated, but no conclusions are reached this day.

In the afternoon, while Lincoln and his wife, Mary, take a leisurely carriage ride past the Navy Yard near Capitol Hill, Booth makes his final preparations.

He arranges his escape and chooses his weapons—a single-shot derringer pistol and a sharp bowie knife.

Lincoln and his wife arrive at Ford's Theatre around eight thirty p.m. with some guests, Major Henry Rathbone and his fiancée. The play, a popular comedy, has already started. The president and his

The presidential box at Ford's Theatre

party are shown to their private box, and the crowd welcomes them with a thundering ovation.

At the same time, Booth is having a drink at a nearby tavern. A customer, recognizing the actor, salutes him with a drunken toast: "You'll never be the actor your father was."

"When I leave the stage," Booth replies, "I'll be the most famous man in America."

DRAMATIC EXITS

Unlike Booth, George Atzerodt, whose job is to kill Vice President Johnson, is no actor. His thin face reveals his worry. He's been drinking most of the day to calm his nerves, which is only making things worse. Although he makes his way to Johnson's rooming house, he doesn't immediately try to find his victim. First he walks into the downstairs bar and orders another drink, and then another. With every sip, he becomes less convinced of the need to assassinate the vice president. Eventually he simply rides away.

Lewis Powell, a former Confederate soldier, has no second thoughts about killing Secretary of State Seward. He talks his way into Seward's house, where Seward is recovering from the accident that occurred the week before, by pretending to deliver some medicine. He fights his way through Seward's sons and another man, then slashes the injured secretary of state's face and neck with his knife, but fails to kill him. Blood is everywhere. Powell escapes into the night.

At Ford's Theatre, the play is in its second hour, and Booth lurks inside the lobby, listening for just the right moment to attack. He hears the line of dialogue he has been waiting for and begins his route to Lincoln's box. He finds the door unguarded. The substitute bodyguard has left his post for a refreshment. Booth slips inside. No one has noticed him.

Booth stands in the shadows behind the president, waiting for one of the actor's to say a certain line that he knows will produce a great explosion of laughter. The line is spoken, crowd roars, and Booth fires his pistol, hitting Lincoln in the back of his head. The president goes limp in his chair as Major Rathbone jumps up in surprise. Booth wounds Rathbone with his knife and leaps from the box onto the stage below. The spur on his boot gets caught in a flag, and he lands awkwardly, breaking his leg. Before anyone in the theater can react, Booth pulls himself up to his full height and calls out, "Sic semper tyrannis" (a Latin phrase meaning "Thus always to tyrants"—the state motto of Virginia).

> **SECRETARY OF STATE SEWARD WILL SURVIVE HIS WOUNDS AND GO ON TO SERVE UNDER PRESIDENT ANDREW JOHNSON.**

He staggers across the stage and escapes through the back of the theater, where his horse is waiting. He heads for a bridge that will take him out of the

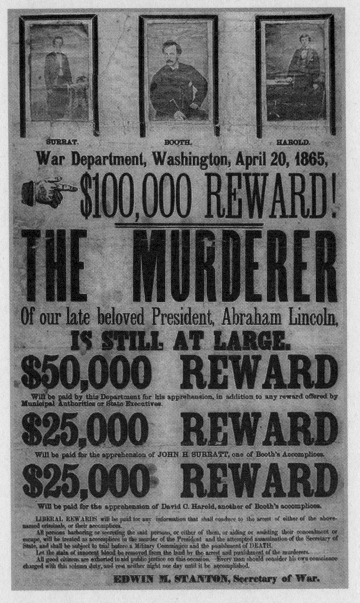

The hunt for the conspirators began immediately.

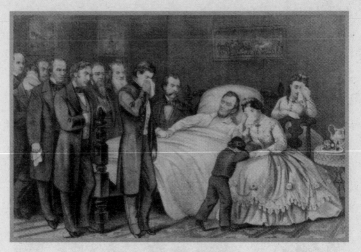

Lincoln on his deathbed

city and into Maryland, which is full of friends of the Confederacy.

As soldiers rush through the theater to the president's box, a doctor in the audience is hoisted directly up from the stage to help Lincoln. He manages to stabilize the stricken leader, but he knows the wound is fatal; it's just a matter of time. Lincoln is carried to a house across the street and stretched out on a bed. He will never regain consciousness. It is eleven o'clock. A death watch begins. When the news spreads,

Washington descends into chaos, just as Booth hoped. A manhunt begins. Soldiers fan out in all directions. Telegraph wires hum, sending reports of the attacks to the rest of the nation.

A team of doctors keeps watch over the president. Mary Lincoln repeatedly enters, screams and faints. The doctors monitor the slow decline of Lincoln's temperature, breathing and pulse. The bullet that drove through his brain is still lodged behind his swollen right eye,

AFTER A TWELVE-DAY MANHUNT IN WHICH HE'S AIDED BY OTHER CONSPIRATORS, BOOTH WILL BE KILLED. MOST OF HIS FELLOW CONSPIRATORS WILL BE CAPTURED, TRIED, AND HANGED.

which turns purple, then black. At twenty-two minutes past seven in the morning, the president lets out his last breath. Secretary of War Edwin Stanton, who's been by Lincoln's side throughout the ordeal, whispers a fitting tribute to a man who, since childhood, hoped to leave an immortal mark on the world: "Now he belongs to the ages." ⑩

1 2 3 4 5 6 7

8 9 → 10 ← 1 2 3

4 5 6 7 8 9 10 1 2

3 4 5 6 7 8 9 10 **12**

3 4 5 6 7 8 9 10

ONE TWO THREE FOUR FIVE SIX

AFTERWORD

DECEMBER 6,
1865

FREEDOM

Washington DC.

To the dismay of both his opponents and his friends, Lincoln believed his job as president was to enforce and defend the Constitution of the United States. That's why he resisted demands from members of his party to immediately abolish slavery. It's why the Emancipation Proclamation had the strange effect of abolishing slavery in former rebel states and territories that Lincoln controlled only by force, while allowing slavery to continue in Union states where he had the most legal authority.

But on this day, eight months after his assassination, Lincoln's personal disgust with slavery and his wish to see it eradicated has finally become part of the Constitution. The Georgia state legislature has approved the Thirteenth Amendment to the Constitution. It's the twenty-seventh state to do so, which means that, as required by law, three quarters of the nation's thirty-six state legislatures have consented to the text settled upon by the U.S. Congress. This is only the third amendment added to the Constitution since the Bill of Rights was ratified in 1791.

The amendment is short and simple:

Section 1. Neither slavery nor involuntary servitude, except as a punishment for crime whereof the party shall have been duly convicted, shall exist within the United States, or any place subject to their jurisdiction.

Section 2. Congress shall have the power to enforce
this article by appropriate legislation.

Because slaves had already been freed in the defeated Confederate states, this amendment, ironically, probably has the greatest effect in Kentucky, a Union slave state. Soon, as many as forty thousand slaves will be freed in Kentucky alone.

TENDER LOVING CARE

Unfortunately, the freed slaves will not easily enjoy all the blessings of liberty. State governments and individuals will find ways to refuse the civil rights of freed slaves.

In this period immediately after the war, President Andrew Johnson, who succeeded Lincoln, is following Lincoln's example of treating generously southern citizens and states. That policy is having mixed results. Many local and state governments in the South continue to avoid extending full rights to African American citizens. White vigilante groups have been formed to harass and sometimes kill freed slaves and the white citizens who are sympathetic to them. Johnson is almost removed from office by members of his own party who want him to be firmer with Southern governments. Although it's impossible to know whether Lincoln would have found himself in the same position, it's reasonable to consider the possibility that his moderate policies would also have allowed these new and more subtle effects of racism to flourish. Not until the civil rights movements of the 1960s, more than one hundred years after the end of the Civil War, would the last legal roadblocks for African American citizens of the South be removed. In fact, the Thirteenth Amendment would not be formally ratified by the state of Kentucky, which rejected it in 1865, until 1976. Mississippi, which also rejected the amendment in 1865, would give its formal (and, of course, merely symbolic) approval in 1995.

But on this day it's a law. That's a start. ➝

The Lincoln Memorial in Washington DC

NOTES AND SELECTED BIBLIOGRAPHY

Angle, Paul McClelland and Earl Schenck Miers. *Tragic Years, 1860–1865: A Documentary History of the American Civil War*. New York: Simon & Schuster, 1960.

Bishop, Jim. *The Day Lincoln Was Shot*. New York: Harper & Row/ Perennial Library: 1964.

Colbert, David. *Eyewitness to America: 500 Years of America in the Words of Those Who Saw It Happen*. New York: Pantheon Books, 1997.

Fehrenbacher, Don Edward, ed. *Abraham Lincoln: A Documentary Portrait Through His Speeches and Writings*. New York: New American Library, 1964.

Goodwin, Doris Kearns. *Team of Rivals: The Political Genius of Abraham Lincoln*. New York: Simon & Schuster, 2005.

Hart, Albert Bushnell. *American History Told by Contemporaries, Volume III: National Expansion 1783–1845*. New York: Macmillan, 1901.

Hart, Albert Bushnell. *American History Told by Contemporaries, Volume IV: Welding of the Nation 1845–1900*. New York: Macmillan, 1901.

Jaffa, Henry V. *A New Birth of Freedom: Abraham Lincoln and the Coming of the Civil War*. Lanham, MD: Rowman & Littlefield, 2000.

Lincoln, Abraham and Don Edward Fehrenbacher, ed. *Lincoln: Speeches and Writings 1832–1858*. New York: Library of America, 1989.

Lincoln, Abraham and Don Edward Fehrenbacher, ed. *Lincoln: Speeches and Writings 1859–1865: Speeches, Letters, and Miscellaneous Writings, Presidential Messages and Proclamations*. New York: Library of America, 1989.

Lincoln, Abraham, Don Edward Fehrenbacher, Virginia Fehrenbacher. *Recollected Words of Abraham Lincoln*. Compiled and edited by Don E. Fehrenbacher and Virginia Fehrenbacher. Stanford: Stanford University Press, 1996.

Lincoln, Abraham and Roy P. Basler, Marion Dolores Pratt, and Lloyd A. Dunlap, eds. *Collected Works of Abraham Lincoln*. Abraham Lincoln Association (Springfield, Ill.)/Rutgers University Press. 1953.

McPherson, James M. *Abraham Lincoln and the Second American Revolution*. New York: Oxford University Press, 1992.

NOTES

DAY 1:
"extraordinary strength of her mind": Goodwin, 47.
"partly on account of slavery": Goodwin, 91
"a boy of uncommon natural talents": Goodwin, 49.

DAY 2:
"the institution of slavery": Goodwin, 91.

"To this day": Grant, Ulysses S. *Personal Memoirs*. New York: C.L. Webster, 1885–86. 22.

"The occupation": Grant, 22.

"the sheerest deception": Lincoln and Fehrenbacher. *Speeches and Writings 1832–1858*, 162.

"like the half insane mumbling": Lincoln and Fehrenbacher. *Speeches and Writings 1832–1858*, 168.

"equally wandering and indefinite": Lincoln and Fehrenbacher. *Speeches and Writings 1832–1858*, 170.

"knows not where he is": Lincoln and Fehrenbacher. *Speeches and Writings 1832–1858*, 171.

"I opposed one War": Goodwin, 122.

DAY 3:

"dark, rainy and gloomy." Hay, John. *Lincoln and the Civil War in the Diaries and Letters of John Hay*. New York: Dodd, Mead, 1939. 234.

"A house divided against itself cannot stand." Lincoln and Basler. Vol. 2, 461-68. See:
http://usinfo.state.gov/infousa/government/overview/22.html

"says that he looks forward": Last Joint Debate, at Alton. Douglas's Reply. October 15, 1858.
http://www.bartleby.com/251/73.html

"Mr Lincoln, following the example": First Joint Debate at Ottawa. Douglas's Speech. August 21, 1858.
http://www.bartleby.com/251/11.html

"I hold that": Third Joint Debate at Jonesboro. Douglas's Speech. September 15, 1858.
http://www.bartleby.com/251/31.html

"It is one thing": Last Joint Debate, at Alton. Douglas's Reply. October 15, 1858.
http://www.bartleby.com/251/73.html

"The fight must go on" Letter to Henry Asbury, Nov. 19, 1858. Lincoln and Basler, Vol. 3.

DAY 4:

"Of strange, discordant": Goodwin, 9.

"destroy the government": Fehrenbacher, *Abraham Lincoln: A Documentary Portrait*, 138.

DAY 5:

"proud to say": Angle and Miers, 7.

"May I be pardoned": letter to John A. Gilmer. December 15, 1860. Fehrenbacher, *Abraham Lincoln: A Documentary Portrait*, 147–148.

"the long continued and intemperate interference…": Jaffa, 170.

"with vague notions": Jaffa, 170.

"Dates of Secession and Black Population" [table]: original table prepared by Prof. John C. Willis of The University of the South (Sewanee). See:
http://www.sewanee.edu/faculty/Willis/Civil_War/tables/dateSecession.html

"The prevailing ideas": Jaffa, 222.

"is suicide": Roland, Charles P. *The Confederacy*. University of Chicago Press, 1960. 30.

"You people of the South": Lewis, Lloyd. *Sherman: Fighting Prophet*. University of Nebraska Press, 1993. 138.

"S.S. Baltic.": Hart, *Welding of the Nation*. 220.

DAY 6:

"feverish excitement": Stephenson, Nathaniel W. *Lincoln: An Account of his Personal Life, Especially of its Springs of Action as Revealed and Deepened by the Ordeal of War*. Indianapolis, IN: Bobbs-Merrill, 1922. 174.

"I say emphatically": Angle and Miers, 6–10.

"the threats of": Livermore, Mary A. *My Story of the War: The Civil War Memoirs of the Famous Nurse, Relief Organizer, and Suffragette*. Da Capo Press, 1995. 86.

"like the first peal": Livermore, 89.

"It is not possible": Lincoln and Basler, Vol 4, 340–41.
  Cited at "The Lincoln Log":
  http://www.thelincolnlog.org/view/1861/4/19
"The day is lost": Angle, Paul McClelland and Earl Schenck Miers.
  The Lincoln Reader. Da Capo Press, 1990. 375.
"In Washington": Whitman, Walt. *Specimen Days*. D. McKay, 1883.
  24.

DAY 7:

"I think to lose Kentucky": Angle and Miers, 153.
"You hold more power": Angle and Miers, 391–392.
"He would look out": Angle and Miers, 389–390.
"I approve of the proclamation": Angle and Miers, 390–391.
"You all remember": recollection of Salmon Chase. Angle and
  Miers, 398–399.
"at the present time": Angle and Miers, 402.

DAY 8:

"short, short, short": Lincoln, Fehrenbacher, and Fehrenbacher.
  Recollected Words of Abraham Lincoln. 46.
"So cold! If only it were alive!": Young, John Russell. *Men and
  Memories: Personal Reminiscences*. In Colbert, 229.
"flutter and motion": Goodwin, 585.
"The central idea": Goodwin, 585.
"Four score and seven": Fehrenbacher. *Abraham Lincoln: A
  Documentary Portrait*. 244.
"Is that all?": Young, 229.
"I should be glad": Colbert, 227.

DAY 9:

"indescribable sadness": Goodwin, 721. Quoting Sen. James
  Harlan.
"sank down in": Goodwin, 719. Quoting John S. Barnes.
"I think we are near": Goodwin, 721.

"General Lee surrendered": Grant, Ulysses S. *Personal Memoirs of U. S. Grant*. New York, 1885. 560.

"with malice toward none": Fehrenbacher, *Documentary Portrait*. 278–279.

"I suppose arrangements": Fehrenbacher, *Documentary Portrait*. 280.

DAY 10:

"Those about the President": Bishop, 108.

"no hanging": Bishop 126.

"You'll never be": Bishop, 182.

"Now he belongs": Bishop, 298.